Many Skies Ha… …n

Magg… …kins

To Jenni

With love

Maggie

x

First published in 2018 by Wild Mouse Press.

Cover illustration by Jon Everitt

Designed and typeset by Jon Everitt

www.joneveritt.net

ISBN 978-1-9999756-9-2

In memory of Janusz Jasicki

(1987 – 2017)

… and others taken by the water

Foreword

'We cannot, after all, judge a biography by its length, by the number of pages in it; we must judge by the richness of the contents ... Sometimes the 'unfinisheds' are among the most beautiful symphonies.'

Victor E. Frankl

Janusz Jasicki, the light of my life, was a man of his own mind – and luckily for me, that mind (and heart) was full of love, kindness, and mischief. He was a man who worked harder than anyone I have ever met. He knew how to play just as hard, whether it be with a group of friends, or off on an adventure, or just the quiet silliness of a relaxing evening at home with me and our pets Wilson and Phoenix.

Janusz adopted Ireland as his home and Ireland adopted him with open arms. His Polish accent combined with his Dublin tones, gave him a distinctive Irish lilt. He always tried to use as many Irish phrases as he could, like 'Good man yourself', or 'It is what it is!'

The seventh son of a family of eight boys, Janusz trained as a chef, and in his younger years arrived in Ireland where he worked in the catering sector in Dun Laoghaire. Janusz returned to Poland for a short while, but Ireland lured him back where he worked for a time in Halfords before starting a career at Fannin Healthcare in 2015 where he was highly regarded by colleagues, managers and customers alike; it says it all that the company had to recruit two people to replace him!

Janusz loved the great outdoors and was a regular along with myself and our dog Wilson in the Wicklow hills. As I told him many many times, he was my home. He will remain forever in our hearts the young, funny, easy going, loveable rogue with a heart of gold.

Cat Sawkins

Contents

Introduction

Many Skies Have Fallen contains poems written as a response to the tragic death of my daughter's partner, Janusz Jasicki, who drowned in the River Shannon in October 2017. Others, written while Janusz was still alive, are included because they relate to my Irish heritage or because they seem to contain a presentiment not apparent at the time of writing. In one of my last memories of Janusz we are playing chess (again) in a holiday cottage on Donegal's Wild Atlantic Way. I never managed to beat him.

Maggie Sawkins

What is Written

One among many,
red leaf
that I troubled

to pick from the ground
in the walled garden
of Strokestown Park.

To the hotel
in Carrick I carried it
to lodge in between

the middle pages
of 'Constance Markievicz',
in whose revolutionary life

I'd hoped to find
distraction.
It was day nine

and the young man, Janusz,
was an absence none
could fathom.

Who knows
what attracts us?
Why we keep searching

when logic
tells us nothing
of the living will be found.

Red leaf,
I don't even know your name.
It was the end

of Autumn. Most things
that were destined
to fall had already fallen.

Abha na Sionainne
(The River Shannon)

My birthplace is a hollow.
From the heights
of Cuilcagh Mountain
I was let loose to fall.
My heart is snowmelt, rain.
I'm the granddaughter
of Manannan Mac Lir,
God of the Sea.
I heard his whisper.
It's in my nature to follow.
I rushed down slopes,
slithered around hills,
meandered the mainland.
The straight and narrow
could not contain me.
I multiplied. Filled lakes
with dancing mirrors.
I think of them as satellites of my soul.
I have named small islands,
that formed around me:
Cow, Duck, Hare, Horse.
Now I seep into bogs and callows.
I have become a bed
for rushes and reeds
for non-breathing things.
I branch out into fingers of skinny rivers:
Suck, Inny, Brosna, Fergus, Maigue.
They will find their own endings.
It's in my nature
to catch the fallen –
to be haunted by the shadows
of moving things.

I have parted my heart
seamless around them.
You cannot condemn me –
I will keep on running
towards the ancient
mouth of the sea.
It is my calling.

Corryolus

We've got to live, no matter how many skies have fallen.
D H Lawrence

Polska fills the air in the café next to the Bush Hotel. There's irony everywhere. Through the steamed-up window men in mud spattered waders wear high-viz vests bearing the words 'Civil Defence'. This morning little red boats ferried men in life-jackets to search the Shannon. A bevy of swans with their cargo of hope sails weightlessly past. A week ago, eight friends had been go-karting in the sticks, had survived the booze-cruise, were cleaning up for the midnight disco. A faint hint of blue. The day is holding. Friends and family, put up for free in a holiday rental, stare at the river. Well-wishers leave boxes of sustenance at the door. A stranger in the street offers a medallion of St Anthony. On the bridge a poster's taped to a bench where people dally. Footage from the drone. Yellow marshes and the tops of trees, here and there some cows, and underneath it all the black water. A man on a cruiser passing Corryolus. The eleventh day. A hand. Blue. Among the rushes. The sky falling.

Striders

You kneel on the bank to cup the water
    because you want to forget

but you could drink half the river and not still
    the stories in your head.

All night it runs
    through you

churning the random
    possessions of the dead.

In fits you imagine the last steps
    of those who loved you

how they ambled
    in the pitch of night

towards what they hoped
    was halfway-home.

You tilt your face
    and there on the river a swallow

is dipping its beak
    to scoop up striders

scuttering across the surface
    of water.

There's a terrible thirst to be found
    in everything.

Find Me

In the ring around a blackbird's eyes, find me.
In a cup of ocean, a patch of sky, find me.

On this the shortest day of winter,
in the persistence of a seagull's cry, find me.

In a blade of grass by a dusty roadside,
in the mating song of a harvest fly, find me.

In the huddle of trees outside your window,
in the moon's gaze and the wind's sigh, find me.

At the top of a sugar loaf mountain –
imagine rainbow wings and fly, find me.

As you cast your breath you'll find the answer
in the place where dreams collide – find me.

Some Place Down the Road a Sorrow

there's more   than one way
of talking   about the future   cocksure
we think   we know   the face
of the picture   on the cards
sometimes I catch   myself
wondering   whether my grandfather
would have left   half his brood
behind   when he boarded the boat
for the port of New York
if he knew   he'd never return
and would we have spent eleven
days of autumn   searching
for the future   in the fields
near the Shannon   if we knew
it would be so   top heavy
with water   sometimes the past
comes bobbing back   last summer
Janusz   the searched-for one
resurrected a picture   of St Patrick
from my grandfather's derelict
homestead   in Dunbeggan
covered in spores   as if
it had waited decades   for the fluke
of being found   but the framed portrait
of my father   handsome
in his slouch hat   never made
the future   due to the day
my mother   smashed it   during
a fight   but we will find beauty
again   in the spiderweb pattern
of a windscreen   splintered
by an errant stone   before the car
swerves to avoid   the unknown

Destination Port of New York
23 December 1929

Even though your name is there
on the SS Cameronia's passenger list:
Regina M Keohane, scholar aged eight,
of sound mind and body,
you were the one sister
left behind in Dunbeggan,
along with your Grandpa's blue cow
and your milk bottle doll.

But if you had gone
I would not have been born.
I wouldn't have spent my life
caught in an undertow,
watching for the feathering of waves,
fighting the weight of an ocean.

American Wake

At the boot-hollowed threshold
seventeen miles from Skibbereen
I listen for my grandfather's
by God I'll make you skip boy
sing-song voice.

At the farmhouse table
where he might have planned
his American dream,
I trace the wood as if I could find
the whorl of his fingerprints
somewhere in the grain.
Then in a tin box I see
the photograph –
his flock of children left
to fend like babes in the wood.

And the tales my mother told me
that once seemed as distant
as another planet,
flash the room – whiting her eyes
like lightning on a star starved night

To My Mother Who Never Touched a Drop

When I meet her in Hourican's Bar
I will bring the picture resurrected
from the derelict farmhouse

last summer. My great Uncle Phil will offer
me a glass. I'll sip the bitter-black and lick
the froth from my lip.

For once my mother will sit in silence –
but not out of spite. When I lean in I'll catch
the Jameson's on her breath.

I'll unscroll the picture and watch
as she scrutinizes the haloed St Patrick
stationed on the top of a mountain

in his emerald gown –
a shepherd's crook in one hand,
pointing at the ground with the other.

And because she is tipsy, my mother
will not recoil at the nest of snakes
gathering around his naked feet.

When the bar empties, I will slip quietly
into the dazed dark, with a box of matches,
a miracle of sobriety.

Peel

one day you'll find yourself
in an old armchair in an old sweater
peeling an apple
                    so slowly
that the peel will unravel in one long spiral
to the floor
          so slowly
you'll forget about going out
without polishing
                    your shoes
that your jacket has lost three
of its four-eyed buttons
          instead you'll sink into the seat
and focus your mind on the beautiful bones
of your feet
          while staring
                    at your naked apple
you'll close your eyes
          and Wilson will pad his way back
into your old kitchen
you'll fetch him a Bonio from the larder
          pour yourself a drop
                              of the Irish
and remember a snatch of the dream
          where you're climbing
                    Croagh Patrick
with your barefoot mother
          if the woman in the chair next to you
wakes with the offer of a Minto
                    you'll refuse
          because you have your apple
and Wilson at your feet
          wearing his little spiral hat

Tethered

this is where the hardy live
on the ledges of island mountains

no walls, no doors
the hardy have no secrets to harbour

their only concern is the falling
of rocks

they're not unlike this albino spider
that's tethered

a home inside the frame
of my attic window

if I had the strength I'd be like them
dangle from the edge and spin

I'd cast off with silver words
balance in a rectangular sky

Why did you Come? Why did you Stay?

(Questions asked of Quarr Abbey Monks)

Because I'm lost inside
the ferry's heartbeat.
Because the sea outside
reminds me
of my father's eyes.

Because I'm returning
to where my baby heart
was set in motion.

Because the sea balances
the ferry in the palm of its hand,
carries me, its trembling cargo
from here to there.

Because when the time comes
I will do as I'm told: look out
for green and white signs,
locate the life jacket's whistle,
and blow.

Because I know now
it's wrong to step outside
during the hours of darkness.

It's wrong to throw lit matches
over the side of the deck.

I stay because I no longer want to go.
I stay because each day is better
than the last.

Unexpectedly, the Sea

swam into me
as I was laying
my life out on the shore
to dry

As far as I know
I know where the path takes me

swam into me
as if
it had found
a door left open

As far as I can see
I can see where the trees end and the sky begins

as if
it had found
the emptiness
it was searching for

As far as I can hear
I can hear the gravel beneath my feet

You don't believe me?
Come closer. Listen
to the echo of its roar

As far as I know
I never betrayed my heart

The Drowners

They will step
into you –
first a toe, then
the ball of a foot.
Some will come clothed,
though most will leave
something behind –
a tell-tale coat,
a pair of shoes.
They will make it
seem easy, as if
they are stepping
into nightfall –
not even you,
nor the eye of a god,
will be able to stop them.
All you can do is slip
momentarily aside,
witness the last
bubbles of breath,
and then
they are yours.
You may wonder
what panacea they think
you possess –
but you'll be out
of your depth.
All you can do
is offer up your home,
knowing that even if
the world tipped
sideways –
words would not spill
from your mouth.

The Unfinisheds

They were bright once
sometimes still
we can see them shine

between a cleft
in a cloud
or in the shattered mirror

of the sun
riding bareback
on the sea

for a moment
they are there
in that place

where
the tide turns
or in the half space

between breaths
and then they return
to settle

their souls
to stay
again

like that
like small dark things
set in amber.

In Good Time

You will pack your suitcase with the few things that haven't been buried or burnt. You'll put on your overcoat and lock the door. You've spent so many days rehearsing, you think at times you may already have gone. Yet you know you must still be here for each morning you see a face in the fisheye mirror which looks remarkably like your own. Your funeral outfit still hangs unworn in the wardrobe, and the suede boots, that didn't have holes in the soles this time last year, are riddled. Just yesterday you noticed fresh coffee rings on the nest of tables, next to a suit of Tarot, a plate of crumbs.

In good time you'll gather up your collection of wishbones -- saving the starling's for the beloved one – he left before us in a storm.

Remains

Is this what happens? The soul,
after leaving the body, wanders down
alleyways searching for something solid
to inhabit, even the heart of a howling dog
in a ruined city, even a leaf, might do.
Or it spends its time staring into windows;
waiting for its shadow to appear.
Maybe it's in a foreign room listening
for a hymn that's yet to be written.

Perhaps it just leaves traces, like notes
in the margins of a book that's found
its way into the hands of someone
blessed with the task of translating.

At the Borders of Sleep

Tonight words
          are clamouring
                    to come in
          but I'm on my guard
I won't open the door

I'm going to float
          like a goose feather
                    in a room
of black silence
          follow the flight

of my breath
          as it rises
                    I could light
          a candle but I might drown
in its roar

As if I Could

(for Cat)

ghost lights skim the sky as you step from sleep
into the tundra

I watch as you lift your hands to the veil of snow – stop
where you stop

shocked into stillness at the sighting of an arctic fox
its fur blue-white

vanishing into the vast outreach
of nothing

back at the lodge I dream your dreams – pray for huskies
to pull you through

come dawn I'll watch as you ready yourself for home
tuck in your rucksack

a jar of yellow cloudberries, a miniature bottle
of strange liquor

after you've gone I'll step out of myself
into the hollows

of your footprints – I will carry the weight
for you

The Emptiness

Then one day you'll carry the whole sack of it into the rain.

You'll carry it past houses with doors flung open
but you won't step in.
You'll carry it past trees
but you won't stop to shelter.

There'll be faded mansions on every corner, with juke-boxes
blaring. There'll be canned laughter, crocodile tears,
but you'll carry on carrying it

past stray dogs lapping in sudden puddles,
past gamblers and loan sharks drowning in pop-up pools,
but you won't fall in.

You'll carry it with your eyes set beyond the horizon,
beyond the glass gaze of the sun

until you find the right spot to cast off your sodden clothes.
And you'll lay down your weight and your shadow beside it
and the rain will drain through you
and the rain will drain through you.

Old Cabbages

'I had to drop the armful in the road.' *Robert Frost*

I had to drop the armful in the road.
It was too heavy for someone made of flesh and blood.

What was I thinking when I let them pile
their load at my door, holding out my arms

as if I were a dumb waiter, and their woes
as heavy as a load of old cabbages?

I had to drop the armful in the road
before I fell. I'd begun to wobble.

It's my fault, I know. I never said a word,
just held out my arms and accepted

their woes as if they were a load of old cabbages,
as if I were a dumb waiter, not a human

formed of gifts and griefs, the same flesh and blood.
I had to drop the armful in the road.

Landings

If only to be a scattering of light –
to inhabit the sea, the sky,

a thrush's egg, the skin of a berry;
to be labelled with the fineness

of cerulean, sapphire, ultramarine, or
simply to be known as slate or steel.

If only a name could contain us –
we could fall for the throat of a harebell,

land on the wing of a Chalk Hill butterfly,
lose ourselves in the heart of flame.

The Handyman

(after Taliesin)

My name is Janusz
I am the seventh son
My patron saint is Bernard of Montjoux

I have dwelt in the mountains
I have dwelt in the woods
I have been your brother
and your blue-eyed boy
I've been a boarder of snow, a wave-surfer
a chauffeur, a chef, a pawn and a king
I have been a run-a-muck runner
a builder of sheds
a fixer of broken things
I've been the wing of a jackdaw
a door left open
a leaf blown in under your feet
I've seen the sun rising over a river
a sun setting over the Mountains of Mourne
I have turned with the hands of a clock
one score year and ten
My home is the arc of a lunar rainbow
the beat of a heart asleep on a moor
My name is Janusz
I am the seventh son
I'm building my ladder of chairs to the stars
I have been dead
I have been alive
All these things I have been

Search Party

We said we'd never come back to Carrick but here we are pitching our tents, well away from the rushes and reeds. Eamon's pulled up in his rally car and here's Len with his smokes and beers, followed by Gavin with a box of torches. Cat's famous lurcher is burying a bone while Luke O'Mahony is flying his drone over a field of meadowsweet. And here comes Menno and here comes Graeme all dressed up in their running gear. St Jerome, with his pen and quill, who arrived last night, is supping his ale and cupping his ear, hoping to translate the river's tale. Even God's shown up with his whoopee cushion and a tome of jokes. There's brother Robert with his sad eyes and, to pass the time, Risk and Twister. And next to the tree, Stacey's setting up a coconut shy. Grainne and Jenny are painting faces while Annett's limbering up for the wheelbarrow race. We said we'd never come back to Carrick but here we are — almost a crowd! Pitching our tents, stitching our hearts, well away from the rushes and reeds.

Thanks

From the friends and family of our beloved Janusz, we are forever grateful to the Lough Ree Sub Aqua Club who searched endlessly for Janusz, alongside the Civil Defence and the RNLI. We will never forget the efforts of each person involved in the search. You will probably never know how much the amazing hard work you put in has meant to us.

Cat Sawkins

Divers of the Lough Ree Sub Aqua Club searched for Janusz after he went missing in Carrick on Shannon on 30 September 2017. It was one of the club's members, Paul Newman, who found him eleven days later.

The Club, from Lanesboro, County Longford, has had more than its share of tragedy since it was founded in 1983, following the drowning of a local man while boating.

A Search and Recovery unit since its foundation, its divers, who hail from several of the surrounding counties, have been involved in hundreds of missions, not just in the Midlands, but across the country.

Club Chairman, Michael Farrell, who first became involved twelve years ago, says they must be ready for a call-out at any time.

"When you come back to the clubhouse from a mission, you get the equipment ready to go again, regardless of the time of day or night. It has to be that way."

Acknowledgements

Poems, or earlier versions of these poems have appeared in the following publications:

Brittle Star, Butcher's Dog, Ferry Tales, Picaroon, Poetry & All That Jazz, South Bank Poetry, The Zig Zag Woman (Two Ravens Press), Zones of Avoidance (Cinnamon Press).

Song extract, Man on the Moon, by REM

Maggie Sawkins won the 2013 Ted Hughes Award for New Work in Poetry for her live literature performance 'Zones of Avoidance'. She lives in Portsmouth, UK, where she delivers creative writing projects in community and healthcare settings.

www.zonesofavoidance.wordpress.com

"Let's play Twister, let's play Risk,
yeah, yeah, yeah, yeah

I'll see you in heaven if you make the list,
yeah, yeah, yeah, yeah."